ISLAM
PROGRESSIVE C...
IN THE 21ST CENTURY IS THE
TOPIC OF OUR TIME
AND
DEFEATING THE THREAT OF
GLOBAL TERRORISM,
IDEOLOGY, ISIS, THE WEST AND
THEIR ALLIES

MR. ATIEAH

Copyright 2017 by Mr Atieah - All rights reserved.

This document is geared towards providing exact and reliable information in regards to the topic and issue covered. The publication is sold with the idea that the publisher is not required to render accounting, officially permitted, or otherwise, qualified services. If advice is necessary, legal or professional, a practiced individual in the profession should be ordered.

- From a Declaration of Principles which was accepted and approved equally by a Committee of the American Bar Association and a Committee of Publishers and Associations.

In no way is it legal to reproduce, duplicate, or transmit any part of this document in either electronic means or in printed format. Recording of this publication is strictly prohibited and any storage of this document is not allowed unless with written permission from the publisher. All rights reserved.

The information provided herein is stated to be truthful and consistent, in that any liability, in terms of inattention or otherwise, by any usage or abuse of any policies, processes, or directions contained within is the solitary and utter responsibility of the recipient reader. Under no circumstances will any legal responsibility or blame be held against the publisher for any reparation, damages, or monetary loss due to the information herein, either directly or indirectly.

Respective authors own all copyrights not held by the publisher.

The information herein is offered for informational purposes solely, and is universal as so. The presentation of the information is without contract or any type of guarantee assurance.

The trademarks that are used are without any consent, and the publication of the trademark is without permission or backing by the trademark owner. All trademarks and brands within this book are for clarifying purposes only and are the owned by the owners themselves, not affiliated with this document.

Table of Contents

Introduction 1

Islam: Main Sects of Islam and their beliefs; 3

Islamic World and democracy in the 21st century 7

The West and their alliance with undemocratic countries in the Islamic world 10

Defeating the threat of global terrorism and ISIS ... 14

  Failed States and ISIS 20

Prophet Mohammed and Western Scholars. 23

IMAM ALI 28

Quran 31

ISIS Ideology (where does it come from and their roots of terrorism); 39

Islam: Terrorism in the name of Islam 42

Islam and inventions 46

Conclusion 51

Introduction

Today we are talking about the most controversial topics of our time: whether Islam is progressive or regressive in the 21st century, defeating the threat of global terrorism, ideology, ISIS, and the West and their allies. In this book, I will discuss these topics above and Islam in a comprehensive way, including all the sects of Islam, and I will prove my arguments with compelling evidence. By investigating the actual sources of Islam, in fact beyond that by discussing all the contributing factors, I will clearly show whether Islam is progressive or regressive in the 21st century, as well as the causes for this. An increase in attacks from Isis on the West has led some to question whether Islam is progressive, or whether this is just a tiny minority that doesn't really represent Islam, just like other groups such as the IRA, Eta, Far-right extremists, and so on.

The phenomenon of terrorism must be defeated, whether it is from terrorist groups like ISIS, AL-Nusra, AL-Qaeda, or even Far-right extremists and their narrative.

Mr Atieah

I will thoroughly examine the effect of terrorist groups like ISIS and AL-Nusra on the world and the West, what the West has done so far to combat these extremist groups ideologies whether by military means or by other means.

Where do these extremist groups get their ideology from? Or are they just brainwashed? I will also try to explain with conclusive evidence whether they indeed got this ideology from somewhere or not. In other words, I will examine if they are just misguided fools by using all the facts today and historically.

Are there polices of the West and their allies defeating terrorism or is it counterproductive with all the facts until the present day?

More importantly, I think it is vital that the world and the West not only defeat these terrorist groups through military action, but also by winning hearts and minds. The media also has a big role in this; we must and we will defeat these terrorists.

Islam: Main Sects of Islam and their beliefs;

Islam to some, or many people depending on your perspective, literally derives from the word 'slam,' meaning peace. There are some who argue that peace is what Islam is all about, but the more important question is whether Islam is progressive or regressive in the 21st century.

In today's world, there are about 1.8 billion Muslims who claim to be Muslim and 'true' followers of Islam, yet they are divided into 5 different main sects, which are as follows: Sunni Islam, Shia Islam, Wahhabism, Sofia Islam, and Hanafi Islam. The last two are both derived from Sunni Islam.

The religion of Islam was believed to be spread by the prophet Mohammed in Mecca and Medina in 610 A.D at the start of the seventh century. Muslims also believe there is only one God and the prophet Mohammed is the last of his messengers. They also believe in all other prophets including Jesus, Moses, Adam, and so on.

Prophet Mohammed, according to Muslims and Islam, is a man who possessed all the attributes of a holy man, as well as the unique qualities which made him a prophet of God and is infallible. Meanwhile, there is a consensus that Mohammed is a prophet for all Muslims, but there is no consensus at all as to the successor of the prophet. Followers of Shia Islam believe that there must be a successor to the prophet, but those of Sunni Islam and other sects of Islam believe that it is not an essential requirement of Islam to have a successor to the prophet.

Shia Islam is based on the doctrine that Imam Ali is the successor of the prophet. In addition to this, they hold the belief that there are 14 Infallibles, including Imam Ali. They are the household of the prophet Mohammed and are the chosen ones; this is a concept held by followers of Shia Islam across the world. The main principals of Shia Islam are the beliefs in the Quran, the day of reckoning, one God, and prophethood. Shia believe they must do the following practices: pray, fast, pilgrimage, Zakat, khums, Amr bil maroof and Nahi anil munkar, Walayah, charity, and mourning of Muharram. Khums means you give twenty percent of your income to charity; you can either do that or give charity instead. Amr bil maroof and Nahi anil munkar means if you see someone doing something really bad you must tell them, and if you can't, then you must at least show disprovable in your heart. Mourning means they mourn their Imam Hussein.

Sunni Islam believe that the prophet Mohammed did not appoint a successor. Rather, they consider Abu Bakr as caliph, and in total four caliphs this is consistent with the Sunni school of thought. Other names include Ibn al khattab uthman Ibn affan and Ali ibn Abi Talib. Sunni Islam beliefs are as follows: one God, prophet, and messengers and the Quran. They also believe they must do the following practices: pray, fast, give charity, and go to Haij, which means visiting Mecca at least once in their lifetime.

Wahhabism began in (1703 -1792) by Muhammad Ibn Abd al-Wahhab in Saudi Arabia. It emphasizes the sovereignty of God. Muhammad ibn Abd al-wahhab was considered to be a religious leader.

Muhammad Ibn Abd al-wahhab and Mohammed bin Saud both agreed to share power, in what is known today as the emirates of Diriyah, which was the first Saudi state. Then they shared power between their families, which remain in place to this present day. They both established the most extreme form of Islam.

Muslims who do not share his view were considered to be Non-Muslims and infidels. As matter of fact, until this day, Shia Muslims are regarded to be evil and non-Muslims.

Their opinion of non-Muslims who don't subscribe to their views are appalling. To say the least, it certainly incites violence characterizing Jews and Christians as evil and enemies.

Islamic World and democracy in the 21ˢᵗ century

Democracy in the Muslim world is an indicator of whether the Islamic world has been or is progressive to at least a certain extent. The following states are considered to be democratic in the Islamic world by the West. Unanimously, they are follows: Turkey, Indonesia, Malaysia, Bangladesh, Bosnia, Kosovo, Albania, Tunisia, Sierra Leone, Iraq, Kuwait, Lebanon, Azerbaijan, Uzbekistan, Tajikistan, Niger, Burkina Faso, Ivory coast, Mali, Afghanistan, Senegal, Guinea-Bissau, Pakistan, Maldives, and so on.

These states are democratic states, although there may be rare instances where human right abuses have occurred. Nonetheless, they are democratic and in general respect human rights. Human rights abuses also occur rarely in some of the democratic states in the Western world. For example, in the United States, there was Guantanamo Bay prison torture, drone attacks, and in 2009 the CIA interrogation program, the abu-ghraib jail in Iraq, and racial profiling, although now this has stopped, capital punishment is still an ongoing problem in the USA. As for those democratic Islamic countries, they have been democratic for some time, excluding Iraq, Tunisia, and Afghanistan, which only recently became democratic.

There are other countries in the Islamic world that have at least some form of democracy.

Media very rarely mentions these facts about the Muslim world—all we hear is of Saudi Arabia, which as I said above has the most extreme form of Islam which is violent. Reza Aslan, a religious studies scholar and author, "stated on CNN to stop saying Muslim countries, as if Saudi Arabia and Indonesia are the same, and Turkey and Saudi Arabia are the same. This is the definition of bigotry".

Democracy in these Muslim countries is certainly a progressive Islam. More importantly, women's rights are respected in those countries. Turkey has seven heads of state more than the United States of America. Women also vote in all of these countries, but that's not Islam. Only when women can't drive in Saudi Arabia that's Islam.

Of course, undemocratic countries on the other side of the Islamic world make Islam regressive, but what is noteworthy is that Islamic countries that are not only undemocratic but also follow the strict Wahhabi Islam sect have not only made Islam regressive, but pose a serious threat to the West and the world.

The West and their alliance with undemocratic countries in the Islamic world

Saudi Arabia is an ally of the West, particularly the United States. It is the most regressive and undemocratic state in the Islamic world, maybe even in the world. Almost every day now we hear a car or suicide boom around the globe in Iraq, Syria, Lebanon, the United Kingdom, France, Germany, Belgium, the United States, Afghanistan, and so on. These attacks have one thing in common. Wahhabi Islam ISIS, al Nusra, and al-Qaeda all follow the extreme Wahhabi sect, which was found in Saudi Arabia. The Wahhabi Salafi sect is still based in Saudi Arabia. Therefore, it is a perfect example of a country that is regressive undemocratic which follows the Wahhabism sect and is the main obstacle to defeating global terrorism that ISIS poses. Wahhabi terrorism goes back centuries almost 1400 years, but it only became clear to some people after 9/11. In fact, a leaf winner from King's College "stated that, according to analysis of the global terrorism data base, at least 95 percent of deaths caused by Islamic terrorism since 2001 were perpetrated by ISIS al-

Qaeda. Wahhabi Salafi jihadists also stated Iran had virtually no direct link at all, and this was also reported by CNN".

Fareed Zakaria, a CNN host, "Added that although Iran had some bad actors in the region, nonetheless they are fighting ISIS, and it is Saudi Arabia that is spreading this hatred and is the centre for terrorism around the world. This is true, even the most recent terror attacks in Manchester, London, Paris, Berlin, and so on. The perpetrators are all from the Wahhabi Islam sect.

And of course, the 9/11 terrorist attacks. The 9/11 commission report (28 pages long) was released by the US Congress confirms that the 9/11 hijackers most likely were helped by high-ranking Saudi Arabian intelligence officers.

Other reliable sources like the *Daily Beast*, an American newspaper, ran an article by senator Bernie Sanders who stated the following: "intolerance is Saudi Arabia's greatest export. In addition to that Bernie Sanders said, "The countries heights religious authority called down to burn down the churches in Arabia. Saudi textbooks call Jews decedents of pigs. Christians are forbidden from wearing crosses, building churches, or bringing in copies of the Bible. How does the world react? Total surrender and utter appeasement. Diplomats pay lip service to human rights while tens of billions in arms are shipped to the kingdom of hate".

Yet despite these facts, the United States and the West consider Saudi Arabia an ally. By this I mean that the United Kingdom and many other countries in the West consider the Saudi government a reliable ally to defeat terrorism. Donald Trump signed $110 billion arms deals with Saudi Arabia. How does that make any sense? Meanwhile Saudi Arabia is killing innocent civilians in Yemen and are one of the main reasons for global terrorism. To some this is being complicit in crime, to others it is a strategic move to help Saudi Arabia against the influence of the Iranians.

The United States of America and the West alliances with Saudi Arabia Wahhabi government can be traced back to the 1930s. Michael R. Dillon, an academic in a Naval post graduate in Monterey California, stated "That Saudi Arabia and the United States have had a long-standing political alliance in the Middle East since the early 1930s. The U.S has demonstrated through various military deployment and informal agreements that it is committed to Saudi Arabia".

"America's foreign policy, since the early 1930s, has protected and protected the Saudi ruling family and refrained from criticizing the monarchy's domestic polices and human record".

United States support for Saudi Arabia sometimes was through indirect wars. In the 1980s, the U.S. armed Saudi Arabia and Iraq to fight the Iranian government, after Iraq invaded Iran.

Of course, the United States argument for supporting other dictators like Saddam Hussein and Saudi Arabia in the 1980s during the Iraq -Iran war, was as Donald Rumsfeld explained it: "the enemy of your enemy is your friend.

Mr Atieah

Defeating the threat of global terrorism and ISIS

Muslims are most affected by this regressive form of Wahhabism Islamic terror. If the media is not reporting these facts more often, this will help the Isis narrative. A USA report stated at least 83 percent victims of ISIS are Muslims, and it could reach up to 97 percent.

When terrorism occurs by those regressive Wahhabi Islamist groups in Iraq, Syria, and Afghanistan almost on a daily basis, these must be reported more often. The counter argument by some is that because of proximity it's not reported. My response is really? Canada and the USA are farther distances from Europe then Syria or Iraq. First and foremost, this will illustrate to Muslims and Non-Muslims that it's not war between Islam and the West, and that it is vital to defeat ISIS propaganda and defeat the threat of terrorism that ISIS poses to the world.

Winning the hearts and minds is crucial, as military action alone is not sufficient.

Darren Osborne, for example, if he was fully aware that this is not a war waged by Muslims against the world, may not have carried out that attack in the London Finsbury Park Mosque. The same for some stupid Wahhabi Muslims; it will make them think twice because the vast majority of victims of Isis are Muslims. Law abiding citizens being run over is what Isis will use as ammunition to say "see, you have no place in Western society."

God forbid if communities turn against each other. Well, that's exactly what Isis wants to happen, not only does it have the potential to make Islam regressive, but the West as well if civil war occurs between Muslims and Non - Muslims.

What also fits with the Isis narrative and makes it more difficult to defeat the global terrorism threat is the threat that Wahhabi ISIS poses to the world—to rule out that the threat of Global terrorism doesn't exist from Non -Muslim individuals or groups around the world, particularly from white supremacist and other Non-Muslim individuals and groups. The lack of use, and emphasis on the word terrorism, when Non-Muslims are the perpetrators is not only unhelpful to dealing with the terrorism, but will increase racism on the bases that terrorism only exists in the Islamic Wahhabi world. Muslims' fear of racism may lead to lack of trust and the fear to be open as a society to isolation and division only benefits ISIS.

The result of this it will make it more difficult to combat terrorism globally. Here are just some of the examples of terrorism that have happened by white supremacists: Craig Stephen Hicks, Anders Behring Breivik, Darren Osborne, Pavlo Lapshyn, Thomas Mair, Adam Purinton, Dylann Roof, Jeremy Joseph Christian, Jared Lee Loughner, Eric Rudolph, Sean Christopher Urbanski, James Harris Jackson, Timothy James Mcveigh, Wade Michael Page, John Salvi, Oscar Morel, Alexandre Bissonnette and so on.

Anders Behring Breivik is a white supremacist from Norway, who killed 77 people and injured many others. His excuse was that he opposed Islam.

Robert Doggart admitted to plotting a deadly attack against an entire Muslim community in New York and as the Independent newspaper stated, "The following day, authorities discovered he had been trying to recruit people to burn down a Mosque in Islamberg, a predominantly Muslim community". He was not labelled a terrorist at all; in fact, he was charged with solicitation to commit a civil rights violation by intending to damage or destroy religious property.

Jeremy Joseph Christian, on 30 May 2017, killed two people who were trying to defend a woman who was wearing hijab from hate speech. The two men who intervened were stomped to death by Jeremy Joseph.

Pavlo Lapshyn, on 29 April 2013, killed an old Muslim man, 82-year-old Mohammed Saleem, in Birmingham by stomping him to death; Lapshyn also attempted three bombings on local mosques.

Craig Stephen hicks killed three Muslim students in the United States in February 2015. The victims were Yusor Mohammed, Abu-Saleh, and Rezan Mohammed Abu Saleh.

Oscar Morel, on 17 August 2016, killed two Muslims in New York outside a Mosque. The New York Post stated the following: The man accused of fatally shooting an Imam and his aid on Queens Street felt a hatred towards Muslims in the days after 9/11 terror attack, as reported by his brother.

Adam Purinton, on 22 Februarys two men because he believed they were Muslims. The two men actually were from India and Non-Muslims.

Sean Christopher Urbanski, on 21 May 2017, stabbed and killed army lieutenant Richard Collins. Sean was charged with first degree murder only.

Thomas Mair, on 16 June 2016, shot and stabbed Jo Cox, the British Labour party member of Parliament for Bately and Spen West Yorkshire, England.

Darren Osborne, on 18 June 2017, drove a van into Muslim worshipers outside a Mosque in the UK. One person died and 11 were injured.

James Harris Jackson stabbed Timothy Caughman, and he also stated he came to New York to kill African American men. He was charged with first degree murder and hate crime but was not labelled a terrorist.

Dylann Roof is an American and a White suprem-acist who shot 9 black people inside a church. He tried to start a race war but was not labelled a terrorist either.

Alexandre Bissonnette, a Far-right-extremist, killed 6 Muslims inside a mosque in Canada. In this case, some of the news outlets said that he was a terrorist.

Jared Lee Loughner in 2011 shot Arizona congresswoman Gabby Giffords and killed six other people. He was an anti-government activist who killed six people and was charged with murder and attempted murder.

David Copeland is a British Neo-Nazi who became known as the London nail bomber after a 13-day bombing campaign in April 1999 aimed at London's black, south Asian, and gay communities that resulted in three people being killed and more than a hundred injured.

Eric Rudolph, an American terrorist, was convicted for a series of anti-abortion and anti-gay motivated bombings.

Scott Roeder, an anti-abortion extremist, on 31 May 2009 murdered George Tiller, a physician, and the list goes on.

I will mention just some of the groups in the past and today including the Lord's Resistance Army Resistance IRA, Eta, and of course that biggest massacre since World War II, the attack against Muslims in Bosnia in 1995 (and yes it was because they were Muslims).

The media asks Muslims whether they condemn ISIS, but does the media ask Non-Muslims to condemn terrorist attacks committed by Far-right extremists? For instance, Darren Osborne, Robert Doggart, Anders Behring Breivik, Dylann Roof and many others who committed atrocities in the name of white people or Christianity and many others. They certainly don't.

Failed states and ISIS

Failed states and war-torn countries like Libya, Yemen, and Syria, have created a vacuum for Radical Wahhabism Islamic terrorists, and in Libya they are the responsibility of the West and its allies. Certainly, as a result of this vacuum, there has been an increase in migration and terrorism around the globe. The world is a more dangerous place and this has made Islam more regressive in those parts of the Islamic world.

Yes, the West was only fully involved in Libya, but there was intervention in Syria also, even though it was to a much smaller extent, as well as this indirect intervention in Yemen by selling arms to Saudi Arabia and providing military assistance to the Saudi government in Yemen until the present day. Does Islam become more progressive or regressive if the West backs Saudi Arabia? Or do we believe what the Saudi government says is their justification is their fighting Iranian influence? Yes, because Saudi influence is better on the world, right? ISIS, AL-Nusra, Al-Qaeda and so on? Well done, Saudi Arabia for your great influence on the world? This is exactly how Islam become more regressive not only in those parts of the world, but also as a threat to Europe. If the

West is backing the most regressive regime in the world, who is responsible for creating the most regressive Islamic Wahhabi terrorist groups in the 21st century?

In Syria, President Donald Trump before he was elected, stated "That Isis is our focus and we don't want to get into war within the Syrian regime; nonetheless he clearly stated on CNN "who the hill is backing in Syria and do we know who they are? We give them weapons and ammunition, so what are we doing to President Bashir al Assad is better than all the other sides. Trump also stated "That historically we back the wrong side I wonder if he was talking about AL-Qaeda. Hillary Clinton on Fox news admits that the CIA helped mujahedeen to defeat the Soviet Union in Afghanistan, and they were successful in her own words, "It was a bad idea to leave those fanatical groups well-trained and with arms because at the time we did not recognize we were so happy to see the Soviet Union fall".

Isis, Al-Nursa, AL-Qaeda, and other extremist groups around the world are still operating in those countries, and some of those terrorists have trained in these places before they perpetrated their barbaric attacks in the West.

Mr Atieah

The perpetrator of the Manchester terrorist attack, Salman Abedi, stayed three weeks in Libya. Alia Brahimi, a specialist in terrorism and political trends in the Middle East and North Africa, stated the following: "The weakness of central authorities -which fractured into two rival governments in 2014 before being joined by a third UN - backed a government in 2016 that led directly to the breakdown of the rule of law, the security vacuum, corruption, economic stagnation, and the empowerment of unaccountable militia, including jihadist groups".

Islam

Prophet Mohammed and Western Scholars

Prophet Mohammed was born approximately in 570 CE in the Arabian city of Mecca; he was an orphan since his childhood, and he was raised by his uncle Abu Talib. He died on 8 June 632 at the age of 40. His father's name was Abdullah and his mother's name was Aaminah.

The opinion of Non-Muslim scholars and historians on Prophet Mohammed is of huge importance, as well as those of political leaders, theosophists, and writers, and they are as follows: Montgomery Watt, George Bernard Shaw, Michael.H.Hart, Karen Armstrong, Sarojini Naidu, Anni Besant, Nepolean Bonaparte, Gandhi, and James A. Michener, they all agreed unanimously that prophet Mohammed never waged wars. In fact, scholars like Karen Armstrong and George Bernard Shaw were among many others who believed not only that he was a great and unique man but the world was a better place with him alive.

Michael H. Hart wrote *in The 100 a ranking of the most influential persons in history in 1978.* On page 33, he stated the following: "My choice of Muhammad to lead the list of the world's most influential persons may surprise some readers and may be questioned by others, but he was the only man in history who was supremely successful on both the religious and secular level."

Karen Armstrong stated the following: "Mohammed was not an apparent failure. He was a dazzling success, politically as well as spiritually, and Islam went from strength to strength. George Bernard Shaw stated the following: "I have always held the religion of Mohammed in high estimation because its wonderful vitality. It is the only religion which appears to me to possess that assimilating capacity to the changing phase of existence which can make itself appeal to every age. I have studied the wonderful man and in my opinion far from being anti-Christ, he must be called the saviour of humanity".

Thomas - Carlyle- Hero's and heroes worship stated the following: "How one man single-handedly, could weld warring tribes and Bedouins into a most powerful and civilized nation in less than two decades?"

"...The lies (Western slander) which well-meaning zeal has heaped round this man (Muhammed) are disgraceful to ourselves only...How one man single-handedly, could weld warring tribes and wandering Bedouins into a most powerful and civilized nation in less than two decades...A silent great soul, one of that who cannot but be earnest." He was to kindle the world; the world's Maker had ordered s".

The following is from Montgomery Watt, "Mohammed at Mecca, Oxford 1953, p.52: "His readiness to undergo persecutions for his beliefs, the high moral character of the men who believed in him and looked up to him as leader, and the greatness of his ultimate achievement – all argue his fundamental integrity. To suppose Muhammad an impostor raises more problems than it solves. Moreover, none of the great figures of history is so poorly appreciated in the West as Muhammad."

Sarojini Naidu stated the following: "It was the first religion that preached and practiced democracy; for, in the mosque, when the call for prayer is sounded and worshippers are gathered together, the democracy of Islam is embodied five times a day when the peasant and king kneel side by side and proclaim: 'God Alone is Great'..."

Stanley Lane -Poole-Table talk of the prophet: "He was the most faithful protector of those he protected, the sweetest and most agreeable in conversation. Those who saw him were suddenly filled with reverence; those who came near him loved him; they who described him would say, "I have never seen his like either before or after." He was of great taciturnity, but when he spoke it was with emphasis and deliberation, and no one could forget what he said..."

Rev Bosworth Smith, Mohammed and Mohammadanism, London 1874 p.92: "He was Caesar and Pope in one; but he was Pope without Pope's pretensions, Caesar without the legions of Caesar: without a standing army, without a bodyguard, without a palace, without a fixed revenue; if ever any man had the right to say that he ruled by the right divine, it was Mohammed, for he had all the power without its instruments and without its supports."

Prophet Mohammed preached Islam with peace and love. If anything, it was those who opposed Mohammed's peaceful message who threatened prophet Mohammed with war, and he was told you must accept our demand or face war.

The companions of the prophet Mohammed suffered severe punishment—"they were placed on burning hot coals. They were forced to lie down on the hot desert and were lashed during the night and the day by the disbelievers at that time. Prophet Mohammed never took revenge on those people, rather he asked his followers to be patient. Always acted in self-defence though it's a big misconception and deliberate lie by others to claim that Mohammed waged wars, all the wars were waged against Mohammed and his followers. Mohammed was an orphan; he lost his mother at very young age and even some of his family turned against because he said the truth.

Prophet Mohammed acted in self-defence in all the battles, including Badr.

IMAM ALI

Imam Ali, as I explained above, is the successor of the prophet Mohammed according to Shia Islam, but one of the 4 caliph according to Sunni Islam. What were Imam Ali views of his influence on the world and Islam?

To answer this question, we must look at his position during his lifetime, his narrations on all aspects of life. The most famous book by Imam Ali which was written by him, was *Title Path of Eloquence or Nahjul-Balagha*.

Edward Gibbon, English historian and writer, in fact considered to be one of the greatest historians, he described Imam as unique and essential to humanity.

These were his exact words "The zeal and virtue of Ali were never outstripped by any recent proselyte. He united the qualifications of a poet, a soldier, and a saint; his wisdom still breathes in a collection of moral and religious sayings; and every antagonist, in the combats of the tongue or of the sword, was subdued by his eloquence and valour. From the first hour of his mission to the last rites of his funeral, the apostle was never forsaken by a generous friend, whom he delighted to name his brother, his vicegerent, and the faithful Aaron of a second Moses". Edward Gibbon The decline and fall of the roman empire, *page 381-2. Or page 885 a new edition in one volume.*

Washington Irving said, "He was of the noblest branch of the noble race of Koreish. "He possessed the three qualities most prized by Arabs: courage, eloquence, and munificence. "His intrepid spirit had gained him from the prophet the appellation of The Lion of God, specimens of his eloquence remain in some verses and sayings preserved among the Arabs; and his munificence was manifested in sharing among others, every Friday, what remained in the treasury."

Thomas Carlyle said, "As for this young Ali, one cannot but like him. A noble-minded creature, as he shows himself, now and always afterwards; full of affection, of fiery daring. Something chivalrous in him; brave as a lion; yet with a grace, a truth and affection worthy of Christian knighthood." [On Heroes, Hero-Worship, And the Heroic in History]

There are many others who historians and experts in all fields believe support this view about Imam Ali; they are as follows: Gerald de Gaury, Sir William Muir, Simon Ockley, Philip Khuri Hitti, and Dr. Henry Stubbe.

Nahjul-Balagha, one of the most famous narrations, "was written in relation to respect, love, forgiveness, happiness, knowledge and is as follows: "you have two brothers in this world, brother in your religion or creation". Meaning that we are all brothers no matter what is our skin, race, religion, ethnicity, and background—what combines all of us is that we are human beings.

On forgiveness, "Imam Ali stated Forgiveness is the best revenge, happiness third rule of happiness do not coerce anyone, no matter how much he wrongs you. "Eighth rule smile even when you are bleeding, the other seven rules can be found on page 55 Path of Eloquence volume one by Yasin T. al- Jibouri ".

"Knowledge is of two types: "one is recorded and one is heard. "What is heard is of no benefit unless it is recorded, and this can be found on the introductory page of Path of Eloquence".

Quran

The Quran is the book that Muslims believe is the word of God or Allah.

Does the Quran promote violence or force people to convert to Islam?

The Quran clearly states, "let there be no compulsion in religion". Author Allama Abdullah yusuf Ali surah AL-Baqra verse 256, page 63

There is also a verse on the Quran, surah Al Ma idah verse 32 below:

"Whoever kills a soul or for corruption done it as if he had slain mankind. And whoever saves one- it is as if he had saved mankind entirely".

Is the Quran anti-Semitic? The answer is below.

"Those who believe (in the Quran) and those who follow Jewish (scriptures), and the Christians and the sabians-anyone who believe in Allah and the last day, and work righteous-ness, shall have their reward with their Lord on them shall be no fear, nor shall they grieve". Author Allama Abdullah Yusuf   Page 14, surah AL-Baqra Verse 62   page 14

According to this verse, the Quran is clearly not anti-Semitic

"O Allah forgive my people for verily they do not know".

The first verse in the Quran always starts with "the name of Allah, most gracious, most merciful.

"He who created death and life, that he may which of you is best in deed: and he is the exalted in might, oft-forgiving": page 844 verse 1 surah Al-mulk

The Quran also clearly emphasizes the importance of equality and justices for women.

Part 4: The family of Imran verse 194 or 195 in other translational books of the Quran and page 113:

"And their lord hath accepted of them, and answered them: Never will I suffer to be lost the work of any you, be he male or female: ye are members, one of another."

In fact, according to the Quran, even if women cheat on married men, be kind and polite and show no hatred, but treat them differently. In other words, your relationship should not be like it was before their infidelity, but don't have hatred. Instead be kind and loving. Read the following verses below and search them for yourself in the translation of the Quran.

Surah women part 4 verse 19 page 120 The holy Quran with English translation by Allama Abdullah Yusuf Ali.

"O.ye who believe! ye are forbidden to inherit women against their will. Nor should you treat them with harshness, that ye may take away part of the dower, ye have given them -except where they have been guilty of open lewdness on the contrary live with on a footing of kindness and love".

Part 4 The family of Imran verse 194 Or 195 in other translation book of the Quran and page 113

"And their lord hath accepted of them, and answered them: "Never will I suffer to be lost the work of any you, be he male or female: ye are members, one of another".

Part 4 surah Women verse 4 page 116 And give the women (on marriage) their downer as an obligation;

The Quran criticizes the believers also. Surah the cow verse 9:

"Fain would they deceive Allah and those who believe, but they only deceive themselves, and realize(it) not".

The verse continues to state verse 10: "In their hearts disease; and Allah has increased their disease: and grievous is the chastisement they (incur".

The Quran praises all good people and is critical of all bad people. The Main requirement is to have a good heart and the intention is vital. In other words, people who have good intentions will go to heaven also, and yes Muslims and believers can go to Hell if they have bad hearts, meaning that bad Muslims or bad people of other faiths who are believers will also go to Hell. The evidence is right above.

This sounds logical to me. Good people with good intentions will go to Heaven. Evil people will go to Hell. Should a serial killer go to heaven or dictators go to heaven? No, some would argue no one should even if somebody kills 1000 people, we should forgive. My question is what about the victims or the families who lost their loved ones? Are they rewarded on the day of judgement because their loved ones lost their lives? God should reward their killers with Heaven, really? Of course not.

The Quran emphasizes the importance of human life

Does the Quran put Muslims on a pedestal?

Although the Quran does clearly states Islam is the right religion, it also clearly states that Christians and

Jews who do good will be rewarded and there is no fear for them. The verses are in the beginning of this chapter. In addition to that, it strongly criticizes bad Muslims and believers also, saying beyond that they will be punished. The argument that the Quran and Islam are anti-Semitic or favours Muslims is completely false.

More importantly, these verses clearly illustrate that people who try to back their argument by referring to the verses used to say that the main idea of Islam is to kill disbelievers is a big lie and taken out of context. The verse refers to a specific period time in history when there was a war waged against Mohammed.

The logical argument is why would the Quran be critical of all bad people, including bad Muslims, meanwhile praising all good people including Non-Muslims like Jews and Christians. The criteria for Islam is pure heart and not to kill the disbelievers.

Pure heart   surah Al- Shuara verse 89 and page 555 The holy translation by Allama Abdullah Yusuf Ali

Verse 89 "But only he will (prosper) that brings to Allah a sound heart".

Others have interpreted very similar

Verse 89 "Except him who comes to Allah with a heart free from evil".

Does the Quran forgive people?

Surah Bowing the knee page 748, verse 14. The holy book with English Translation by Allama Abdullah Yusuf Ali

Verse 14. "Tell those who believe to forgive those who do not hope for the days of Allah; it is him to recompense (for good or ill) each people according to what they have earned".

"O Allah forgive my people for verily they do not know".

There are many Non-Muslim scholars, historians, authors, all of them commended the Quran and they are as follows, Arthur J. Arberry, Gustave Edmund von Grunebaum, Margaret Marcus (Maryam Jameelah), Sir Hamilton Alexander Rosskeen Gibb, Dr. Josef Horovitz, Professor Arthur John Arberry, Jules La Beaume, Prof. Rev. Harry Gaylord Dorman, Dr. Charles Francis Potter, George Sale a British orientalist.

Gustave Edmund von Grunebaum a historian stated the following "The effect of the literary advance which the Koran marks is heightened by a number of passages of sublime beauty. Many of the lines that seem rather commonplace to us must have been astounding and stirring to the contemporaries. But at all tunes will this simile of the Lord and the mysterious aloofness of his splendor penetrate to the innermost heart".

Margaret Marcus (Maryam Jameelah "The miraculous character of the Koran relates not only to origin and contents but to form. How could an unschooled man produce such a work that is not only insuperable but inimitable? Even if men and jinn were to collaborate, they could not produce the like of it. Muhammad was authorized by God to challenge his critics to produce even one comparable Surah."

Islam and Orientalism, Margret Marcus (Maryam Jameelah), pg. 34; Muhammad Yusuf Khan & Sons, 1981

Sir Hamilton Alexander Rosskeen Gibb "But the Meccans still demanded of him a miracle, and with remarkable boldness and self-confidence Mohammed appealed as the supreme confirmation of his mission to the Koran itself. Like all Arabs they were connoisseurs of language and rhetoric. Well then, if the Koran were his own composition other men could rival it. Let them produce ten verses like it.

If they could not (and it is obvious that they could not), then let them accept the Koran as an outstanding evidential miracle."

Arthur. J. Arberry who was a non-Muslim scholar; he translated the Quran into English.

Dr. Josef Horovitz "The Qur'an played a key role in the intellectual development of intellectual development of Muslims.

It motivated them to focus upon scholarly research and instigated the creation of knowledge. Even their formidable military advances, that led them to the very heart of Europe, were inspired by the Qur'an".

"There, in a time when all of Europe languished in the Dark Ages, the Muslim nation was responsible for lighting the torch of humanity and knowledge. It was then that they rendered such great services to all field of science and learning".

ISIS Ideology (where does it come from and their roots of terrorism);

The ideology of ISIS—do they get it from somewhere? They do indeed get it from Yazid and Muawiya, both were Wahhabi Muslims. Their history was very brutal and bloody; not only were they dictators and barbaric killers, but they would behead people including Imam Hussein the grandson of the prophet Mohammed. The policy of Yazid, as well as Muawyia, was to be in power at whatever cost, by paying money to his followers' deception in the name of Islam. By reading the Quran, they would tell people to follow them as they were the only real Islam.

People at that time would be forced to follow their ideology or face death, isolation, and poverty, which also would kill people as result of death because of poverty. In one of Muawiya's statements in his will before son Yazid became his successor, he said: "I have paved the way for a government for devil and sinner like you".

Yazid committed many atrocities but his biggest atrocity was against Imam Hussein, the grandson of the prophet Mohammed. Imam Hussein was told consistently to give his allegiance to Yazid, or face severe consequences. The same was sent to him before the battle began.

Imam Hussein refused Yazid's message and would not accept his allegiance. Yazid threatened with war and atrocity. Imam prepared to defend the true Islam to protect his followers and family.

The Battle of Karbala took place on Muharram 10, in the year 61 AH of the Islamic calendar (October 10, 680 AD) in Karbala, in Iraq. The battle took place between a small group of supporters and relatives of Muhammad's grandson, Husayn ibn Ali, and a larger military from the forces of Yazid I, the Umayyad caliph.

Yazid followers burned the tents of the family of Imam Hussein; they were so brutal they killed Imam Hussein's infant son with arrows aimed at him.

Then shimr killed Imam Hussein and was decap-itated. Imam Hussein even in the last second said, "I fear before he passed away. I fear for you and in tears told him don't do this I fear your will go to hell if you do this.

The history is simply repeating itself, Wahhabi terrorism against Muslims mostly and sometimes against Non-Muslims.

Historians

4-Mahatma Ghandi "I learned from Husayn how to be wronged and be a winner."

Antoine Bara: "No battle in the modern and past history of mankind has earned more sympathy and admiration as well as provided more lessons than the martyrdom of Husayn in the battle of Karbala."

Islam: Terrorism in the name of Islam

History teaches us an important lesson. It helps us understand the role of Islam as a religion, but we must be honest and compare it with other religions like Christianity and Buddhism. Has Islam been more violent than, for example, Christianity and other religions, in the past or today.

Here are the facts: are these groups or people Muslims IRA, Eta, Hitler? Hitler was born from a Christian family. There are also quotes where he talks about Christianity. There are many other crimes committed by Christians which are as follows: Crusades, Inquisition, Holocaust, American slavery, Native American slaughter, and the Lord's resistance army in Uganda.

More importantly, some of them were done in the name of Christianity or in some cases in the name of white people. Mine kampf

Adolf Hitler stated the following: "Today I believe that I'm acting in accordance with the will of the Almighty creator: by defending myself against the Jew I am fighting for the work of lord".

Islam

People argue that was history a long time ago. Ok, history teaches us very important lessons so we learn from it, but even recently too. Let's start with the most recent attacks by white or Non-Muslims in the name of white people, Christianity, and God: in the USA, there was Dylann Roof, Jeremy Joseph Christian, Robert Doggart, Anders Behring Breivik, and so on with details above.

Jeremy Joseph, on 30 May 2017 believed that he was defending Christianity. His attack was aimed against two Muslims women who didn't die thankfully, but sadly the two great American Christians who tried to stop this terrorist after he was bothering these two Muslims women did die. They represent American values, God bless their souls. Dylann Roof committed his atrocity because he was defending white people in his view.

Robert Doggart, in the name of God, tried to kill an entire Muslim community in the United States and many others committed similar acts as well.

My main argument is about how the media reported these terrorist attacks. Did they say breaking news on Fox News, white man or Christian tried to kill Muslims or black people in the church in the name of white people, or Christianity?

Or did Fox News and other news outlets make the following statement: we must do something about this white community or Christian community to stop this hatred. No, these guys are doing it in the name of Jesus. In fact, Fox News presenter Eric Bolling stated "zero terrorist acts have been committed in the name of Christianity, and Muslims have always killed in the name of Islam". Fox News is fair and balanced, right? The same goes for some other channels.

Right now, Christians are massacring Muslims in central Africa, but where is the media criticism of radical Christians?

The biggest massacre since World War II occurred against Bosnia in 1995, but did anyone in the media question the Christian faith? Absolutely not.

Buddhism has also committed atrocities of this sort. In fact, they are still committing atrocities in Myanmar against Muslims.

Does that mean Christians are by nature violent because some terrorists act in the name of Christianity? Absolutely not, Christians and Non-Muslims have also achieved great things for the world, and the vast majority are peaceful and loving people.

Islam

We should apply the same rule to Muslims when a select few perpetrate terrorist attacks in the name of Islam, and in fact falsely point to their prophet as a violent man when all historians believe he was a loving man.

Islam has contributed amazing things to the world, either in the past or even in some instances today.

Islam and inventions

There are Muslim inventors and influential figures, Scientists, space explorers, Nobel prize winners, sports stars, so on. This is of huge importance because it clearly shows that Islam is progressive to at least certain extent today and even in the past, and this is a positive contribution from the Islamic world.

Here are a list of some of the influential Muslims: Jawed Karim, Ali Javan, Farouk El-Baz, Anousheh Ansari, Sultan Bashiruddin Mahmood, Muhammad Ibn Musa al-Khwarizmi, Ismail al-Jazari, Muhammad Ali, Malcom x, Jabir Ibn-Hayyan, Ibn Rushd, Ibn al Haytham Ibn Sina, Jamil Sidqi al-Zahawi, Alhazen(Abu al Hasan, and Grand Ayatollah Sistani, Mohamed Elbaradei, Malala Yousafzai, It is also worth noting that the first hospital was invented in Egypt.

Jawed Karim is an American internet entrepreneur who co-founded YouTube and was first person to upload a video on it.

Ali Javan, an inventor, was the first inventor of a gas laser. He died in 2016.

Islam

Farouk El-Baz, a space scientist, worked with NASA to assist in the planning of scientific exploration of the moon.

Sultan Bashiruddin Mahmood "is a Pakistani nuclear engineer and a Islamist scholar on Islamic studies".

Mostafa El-Sayed is a leading nanoscience researcher, and was awarded a priestly medal in 2016 by King Langmuir.

Anousheh Ansari, on 18 September 2006, was the first female explorer from a middle eastern background and is Iranian American Muslim. She is also an engineer.

Muhammad Ibn Musa al- Khwarizmi "is a Persian mathematician, astronomer one of the fathers of algebra, geographer, and scholar in the house of wisdom in Baghdad".

Ehab Abouheif is an artist and scientist. He was awarded a fellowship for Natural Sciences in US and Canada. Dake university.

Ismail al-Jazari was born in 1136 in Cizre, Turkey. In 1206, "He" invented an early crankshaft with a crank-connecting rod mechanism in his twin-cylinder pump".

"He is a scholar, polymath, inventor, mechanical engineer, artist, and mathematician".

Ibn Sina was a polymath who is considered to be one of the most significant thinkers and writers of the Islamic golden age.

Ibn Rushd Polymath, "wrote on logic, Aristotelian, and Islamic philosophy, theology, the Maliki school jurisprudence, psychology, politics, and Andalusian classic music theory, geography, mathematics, and the mediaeval sciences of astronomy, physics, and celestial mechanics".

Jabir Ibn-Hayyan, "also known by the Latinization Geber, was a prominent polymath: a chemist and alchemist, astronomer and astrologer, engineer, geographer, philosopher, physicist, and pharmacist and physician. Born and educated in Tus, he later travelled to Kufa. He is sometimes referred to as the father of early chemistry".

Jamil Sidqi al-Zahawi, was a poet and philosopher and was an advocate for women's rights. He died in Baghdad in January 1936.

Ibn al Haytham Was "Muslim, scientist, mathematics astronomer, philosopher. He is known today because he made crucial contribution to the principals of optics, astronomy, Mathematics and visual perception. He also was first to invent pin hole camera and Camera obscura".

"He is considered to be the father of optics." He was the first to explain that vision occurs when light bounces on an object and then is directed to one's eyes".

Nobel prize winners Malala Yousafzai, Muhammed Yunus, and others in the Islamic world.

Grand Ayatollah Sistani in Iraq was considered to be the most important influential figure to establish democracy in Iraq in 2006, and to stop the bloodshed in Iraq. In fact, Paul Bremer stated, "although he refused to meet with him, his vision for democracy for Iraq was vital".

Mohamed Elbaradei, won the Nobel prize in 2005.

Malcolm X, was a civil right activist he died 21 February 1965.

Muhammad Ali was an American professional boxer and activist. Generally regarded as one of the important sports figures of the 21st century.

Mohamed Farah was a British distance runner. On the track, he mostly competed in over 5000 metres and 10,000 metres, but has run competitively from 1500 metres to the marathon.

Amir Khan is a British professional boxer- he is a former unified light weight world.

Zine dine Zidane, a retired French footballer, currently is the manager of Real Madrid. His position was an attacking midfielder for France national team. He was one of the best players of all time.

Conclusion

Conclusion there are several factors to determine whether Islam has been progressive or regressive in the 21st century, and in determining what impact it has on defeating the war against terrorism, the West and their allies, ideology, and if there is a clear correlation between all of these factors.

Democracy in the Islamic world is a factor used to judge whether Islam is progressive today, and that has helped to a certain extent to defeat the Global threat of terrorism from Isis and their ideology.

The lack of democracy has made Islam regressive in the 21st century, but not necessarily a threat to the West. Islamic countries that are undemocratic and follow the Wahhabi sect and failed states like Libya have not only made Islam regressive in the 21st century but also a direct threat to the whole civilized world, and the world is more dangerous and vulnerable to terrorist attacks. In Libya, Salman Abedi, a Wahhabi terrorist trained 3 weeks in Libya, before he killed innocent civilians in Manchester. Saudi Arabia created ISIS, al-Qaeda, and are responsible for 9/11. As result of all this, it become more difficult to win the war against terrorist groups like ISIS and their Wahhabi ideology. Nonetheless the West and their allies have supported this undemocratic Wahhabi Islamic country pre-9/11. In fact, since the 1930s and until today Saudi Arabia and the United States and some other European allies, consider each other allies.

There has been an increase in terrorist attacks around the world including the West, because of this Wahhabi Islamic ideology. Wahhabi Islamic terrorism, which can be traced back 1400 years ago, show that Muawiyah and YAZID are both Wahhabi Muslims.

The West, including the USA, are partly to blame for the rise of this form of regressive Wahhabi Islam, and Muslims are also partly to blame for this form of regressive Wahhabi Islam in those parts of the world. Surely Muslim communities could not be blamed for the West selling weapons to Saudi Arabia pre-9/11 and providing military assistance in Yemen to the Saudi Arabia today. That makes them complicit in their crimes in my view and others, or failed states like Libya.

Other factors that clearly illustrate that Islam and Muslim are in fact progressive, is that the vast majority of Muslims are on the frontline fighting ISIS, and Islamic countries are victims of ISIS.

There are those who counter this argument by saying ISIS are Muslims. My question is if the IRA, ETA, Far-right extremists, white supremacists, abortion clinic bombers in the USA, Lord resistance army in Uganda, and many others are Muslims? Of course not. In addition to that, many of those terrorist groups which are NON-Muslims have committed crimes in the name of the white race or religions. As well as in the past for example, with Hitler, the crusaders, and so on.

This is exactly what also fits with the ISIS narrative and is a counterproductive method to defeating terrorism, as well, is to never ask non-Muslims to condemn terrorism done in their name of religion or race, while also asking Muslims to condemn terrorism done in their name.

The history of Islam is a major and essential factor that will show us whether Islam has been progressive or regressive in the past or even today, include the fact that Muslims were the first to have a positive contribution to the world. By this I mean maths, numbers, algebra, algorithms, and other inventions, for instance crankshaft, pinhole camera and so on with full details above.   algebra

Of course, the history of Wahhabi Islam only and not other sects of Islam has had nothing to offer apart from murder. This was true 1400 years ago and still today.

Those who argue Islam has always been slow are dishonest. Just some of the examples are as follows: the crankshaft, toothbrush, and shampoo were first discovered by Muslims and were introduced to Europe by Muslims.

Today YouTube founder Jawed Karim a Muslim, Ali Javan Inventor, sultan Bashiruddin Mahmood, samar mubarakmand, Jamil Sidqi al Zahawi and so on with full details in the previous pages of this book.

Yet there are some who say Islam has always been slow, although really, they were the first to make positive contribution to the world. What does that make the West if they took a lot of the positive contributions from the Islamic world slower than slow.

As for those who counter this argument, by stating Islam countries are generally slow today, and yes that is true to a certain extent, it is only partly because of Muslims, but without a doubt it is also partly because of the West colonization that is history, and support for Arab dictators until now.

The West, United States have supported in the past since 1930 s and today Arab dictators for example Saddam Hussein, Hosni Mubarak, Saudi kings until present. How is the Muslim world supposed to develop when the most basic essential need for a civil society to progress is freedom to think, or participate in Elections is that just their fault?

Or is just purely Muslim fault Libya that Libya is a failed state now? Where terrorist groups have been able to provide training and arms to Islamic Wahhabi terrorist around the globe.

Of course, that does not mean at all the West is just to blame. In fact, the West and United States have brought freedom and liberty to the world and parts of the Islamic world. The United States of America and the West liberated Muslim countries like Bosnia, Iraq, Afghanistan, Germany from the Nazi party, and other countries around the world.

The West has been in some cases a force of good without a doubt, in other cases unfortunately a force of evil.

It is equally preposterous to say it is all the fault of Islam, that those countries which are regressive or Wahhabi in some parts of the Muslim world are undemocratic. Tunisia, and other Muslim countries that are now democratic, developed because the Muslims refused regressive Islam. What was the Arabic spring all about? What about those other democratic

Muslim countries that are progressive, and have been democratic for some time? For instance, Indonesia, Turkey, and many others.

That shows that Islam and Muslims countries have either been democratic, or recently been democratic, want democracy like everybody else. More importantly, it shows Islam is compatible with democracy and human rights.

Islam has also been fighting Isis particularly in the democratic Muslim countries, and even in some cases non-democratic countries have been fighting Isis with or without United States of America.

However, the lesson to learn in the past and today is that supporting Arab dictators, AL-Qaeda, and failed states like Libya have led to an increase in terrorist Wahhabi Islamic groups, whether it was pre-9/11 with Saddam Hussein and Hosni Mubarak, and even until the present day Saudi Arabia is our number one ally.

This without doubt has been and is counterproductive today in defeating terrorism.

The way to win this battle in my humble view, is first and foremost to become tough with those states and honest with where this terrorism is coming from.

It is without a doubt the Radical Wahhabis Islam, not radical Islam, that would include all sects of Islam, but at the same time admit that the West must be partly responsible for supporting the Saudi state, Al-Qaeda, and leaving a vacuum for terrorists to operate in failed states like Libya. In addition to that the West is partly responsible for the backing of so-called moderate rebels in Syria, which even Donald Trump recognized before he became the President Trump clearly said "Bashir AL Assad is to me better than those other groups and we are backing the wrong side I provided more details about this in the beginning chapters of this book.

Secondly, we must engage with the vast majority of Muslims as they are the victims of this terrorism and focus primarily on them when discussing Islam and Muslims, not only on the tiny minority Wahhabi radicals.

Thirdly, we must have honest discussions about Islam which are not bias based on Radical Wahhabi Islam. When discussing Islam and the Quran, people tend to ask if the Quran and Mohammed were all about violence. Historians, Scholars Karen Armstrong George Bernard Shaw, and many others agree unanimously that he was a unique and wonderful peace-loving man.

Fabrication of these historical facts is done intentionally to fit with the ISIS narrative, to show that Islam is and Muslims are by nature more violent than other religions, which is of course completely false.

My question is why not even one news outlet ever mentions these facts, that Scholars like George Bernard Shaw, Karen Armstrong, and many others know to be true. They clearly state that Mohammed was a peaceful man and loved to challenge those who claimed Mohammed and the Quran was bad.

I mentioned this in the beginning chapters of this book in full details about Quran verses, pages, and Mohammed roles with compelling evidence that it was positive to society. Of course, the answer to this is that they never do. The media only discusses verses that are taken out of context.

In contrast, does anyone in the media talk about the fact that *Christ said I did not come to bring peace, but a sword*, and Jesus is mentioned in the Bible doing some very violent things? That is written in the Bible, but do they say that's Christianity for you? And do they try to explain it by saying this is why we have Far-right extremists or white supremacists, Hitler, and many others? Do you, Fox News? Fair and balanced, right? Therefore, white supremacists or Christians are by nature more violent? Absolutely not. Which of course is a completely stupid argument as well.

Christianity is a great religion, and so Jesus is a great man, and so is Islam apart from Wahhabi Islam.

To defeat the global threat of Wahhabi terrorism or even Far-right extremists, we must defeat their narrative. In my view, we need to hear the media people talk more about moderate Muslim and Islamic countries that are democratic to illustrate there are democratic Muslim countries that are also Islam. But no what we hear most of the news outlets talk about is ISIS and what they say ISIS is doing in the name of Islam, so therefore that's all of Islam.

We must be either equally critical of all other religions and other groups when terrorism is committed in their name or race, or not.

As for those who counter this argument by stating that ISIS has killed many more, this is why we discuss the history of violence in Islam and the Quran, but not the History of Christian violence and the Bible. Actually, at present in the United States, white supremacists have killed more, according to the polls, as well as the FBI, since 9/11.

In addition to that, historically Non-Muslim groups like the IRA or dictators (like Hitler) killed many more people than Muslims historically have ever killed. Even today ISIS is in the United Kingdom and Germany. There was never a time when the media to tried to connect at all the actual sources of Christianity to the violence committed by those Non-Muslims groups or tyrants, e.g. White supremacists, Myanmar killing Muslims, Central Republic Africa, to the Christian or Buddhist faith, or any other religion, except for Islam.

My question is what do people in America or FOX news, say, or the American people of Christian faith need reformation because of white supremacists or what Christians are doing to Muslims in Central Africa, or the Myanmar Buddhist religion? It needs reformation now or even historically.

Does the media's sole focus on Islam need reformation in America? When it is a fact that white supremacists killed more than Muslims Wahhabi terrorists, when there is also massacre against Muslim in central Africa, they only focus on Islam as religion.

This only helps the ISIS Wahhabi Islamic ideology, to demonize Islam and not to focus on all sects of Islam.

We need to discuss all the facts around the globe, or do we just want people to share the same view of Islam that ISIS and Far-right extremis have of Islam?

Those Non-Muslim groups and tyrants like Hitler read the Bible to justify their barbaric acts. However, the media talks about Islamic history of violence and explain why ISIS and Islam are always violent. More importantly, it is based on fabrications about the founder of Islam. The full details of historians' views on Mohammed are in the beginning chapters of this book.

ISIS has killed many more Muslims than Non- Muslims. That's right, but that's not mentioned often either. Why? If it is mentioned more it will show to the world that this is not war between Muslims and Non - Muslims, and that's crucial in order to defeat ISIS narrative.

Despite this I still think Wahhabi Islam, and not Sofia Islam or Shia Islam, is the biggest threat to the world, even more then white supremacists. This may sound like a contradiction but it is not. When I say white supremacists have killed more than Wahhabi Islam, and while this is true in America and Europe, I'm still questioning the logic and the reasoning of the media to equate this with the entire religion of Islam. For example, the media calls this war against Radical Islam, but it is not—it is against radical Wahhabi Islam. And some in the media use this to spread lies about the Quran, Mohammed, Islam and Muslims celebrating 9-11, and all other sects of Islam.

What also helps the ISIS narrative is to ban Muslims from entering the United States of America solely based on their religion, as it undermines everything that America stands for and it this does not make America great. Those who say that Islamic Wahhabi ISIS has committed atrocities, yes that is true, but by that logic shall we ban Non-Muslims, meaning white people, from entering the United States because of white supremacists who have also committed terrorism against Muslims and Non-Muslims in the name of white people or Christianity? Of course not, that would not make sense either.

I have a question: what about Wahhabi Saudi passengers, or let me guess they are welcome in America, or do they get an upgrade? I wonder is it because they are rich? Or is it because 15 of the 9/11 hijackers were Saudi nationals. Yes, that makes America great again.

Fourthly, the United States and the West should completely reconsider their alliance with Saudi Arabia as the number one ally to win the war against Wahhabi terrorism.

That does not necessarily mean they would have to cut all ties with Saudi Arabia, although that would not necessarily be a bad thing.

I mean if the United States it serious about fighting radical Wahhabi Islam, then on that basis American officials should publicly not only label the Wahhabi Saudi state as a terrorist but confess they are the biggest problem in the Middle East.

In fact, they ought to go beyond that and at least threaten them with sanctions and definitely not sell more arms to the Saudi regime.

They use those arms to either kill Non-Muslims or kill Muslims in Yemen and around the world, and preach hatred against the Muslim world and the West.

Fifthly, the ideology does exist. It is from the Wahhabi school which can be traced 1400 years ago, but nobody in the Western world states this fact clearly.

This is an honest, accurate, and specific description, but instead they apparently give a deliberately unclear slogan, or label it as radical Islam, which is not specific or really true, as it is in fact radical Wahhabi Islam.

This Wahhabi Islamic ideology is the biggest cancer in the world, not Muslim communities. History and historians prove this, their leader was Yazid and Muawiya, and they killed the prophet's grandson Imam Hussein, because he opposed their barbaric and violent ideology.

Imam Hussein, the grandson of the prophet, is mostly mourned by Shia Islam, although they are some moderate Sunnis who also mourn his death each year. Wahhabis never do this, and they consider Shia Muslim and other peaceful Muslim sects to be infidels because they have different beliefs than them.

Sixthly, the West can focus on the progressive Muslims and Islamic countries and their contribution to the world in the past and today to defeat ISIS Wahhabi ideology.

However, if the West focuses only on regressive Muslims like Wahhabi Islam and ISIS and paint Islam with that one brush, that is without a doubt a bad strategy, and won't win hearts and minds in my view.

Instead, it will only embolden Far-right extremists and ISIS sympathisers, as they both share the same view about Islam.

Seventhly and lastly, I have done a comprehensive investigation into the Actual source of Islam, the Quran, and the founder of Islam Mohammed, by referring to actual historians and many of great influential figures. They all conclude the founder of Islam Mohammed was a peaceful and loving man. This is why Islam has been in the past and even today remains progressive.

Those who claim Islam is not a progressive religion because of what the minority of Wahhabi Muslims do, yet at the same time state the vast majority of Muslims are progressive are contradicting their own argument.

How can you base your argument on what a small minority of Wahhabi Muslims do, and say that is Islam? What religion does the vast majority of Muslims follow? Christianity? Of course not.

To say the vast majority are progressive Muslim people, and the minority are not, suggests that Islam is a bad religion. Well here is my question to them: then why do they base their arguments only on what the minority of Wahhabi regressive Islam sect do?

Why do they also make false allegations about the founder of Islam, Mohammed? Have they not read the historical facts written by historians or influential thinkers like Ghandi?

Have they not read what author Michael Hamilton Morgan book *Lost History The enduring legacy of Muslim scientist, thinkers, and artists*? Michael

Hamilton stated the following: "When learning about Muslim scholars of the past, it is easy to be amazed by their brilliance, accomplishments and contribution to the modern world. "Each provided a lasting legacy that changed the world in their time and today. One scientists in particular stands above the rest. He is Ibn AL Haytham, the great polymath who lived from 965 to 1040".

Have they also not read what historians and authors like Daniel David levering wrote about the Islamic positive contributions to the West? "There would be no renaissance, no reformation in Europe without the role played by Ibn sina, Ibn Rushd, He is also very critical of the Wahhabi regressive Islam, who have a historical alliance with the West, and their allies that's partly why Islam has not been more progressive.

These are facts, so when Muslims say that the Islamic world is in general slow partly because of the West support for Arabic dictators, it is a fact.

More importantly, there are Muslim democratic countries that show Islam and Muslim are not less human or more stupid, and that show Islam is compatible with the democracy. Even undemocratic Islamic countries don't pose the threat that Wahhabi Undemocratic Islamic countries do.

Islam

Undemocratic Islamic countries, particularly Wahhabi Islamic countries, make Islam regressive without a doubt, but my question is why only focus on the undemocratic countries or undemocratic Wahhabi Islamic countries? Particularly when the West is partly to blame.

Yes, Muslims are also partly to blame, particularly the Wahhabi Islam, absolutely, but what I mean is when you blame everything on Islam and Muslims that Islam is regressive, it's a false argument also. Historically that's not correct.

Other false arguments which are proven to be wrong historically and today are that Islam always has always been slow. In fact, even today Muslims still have scientists, influential figures, Nobel prize winners, YouTube stars, and even sports stars.

Hadiths: Not all hadiths are accurate, in fact according to Islamic law there are hadiths which are false. By this I mean bad Islamic books that have been written by Wahhabi Muslims, and the Wahhabi school solely rely on them to justify their barbaric acts, which is why Wahhabi Islam is a disaster for the whole world

Nahjul-Balagha or Path of Eloquence and other sources are reliable books according to other Islamic schools, apart from the Wahhabi school which has a different opinion than every other sect of Islam.

The first rule of Sharia is the law of the land, by this I mean the law of the country you live in is superior to any law. Including Sharia Law, apart from Wahhabi, they believe their law is first. Sharia also means prayer, fasting, and helping your neighbour, so when the media asks Muslims do you support Sharia, they need to be more specific about what Sharia is.

Jihad means to strive or the right to self-defence. Wahhabi Jihad means attack someone who disagrees with you. Surah in the Quran The Romans, page 606, verse 14. Allama Abdullah Yusuf Ali, which would illustrate one of the meaning of Jihad means to strive.

Therefore, the Wahhabi sect of Islam, is as follows: regressive, undemocratic, having a terrorist ideology, an ally of the West, and one of the main reasons why we have global terrorism today. It is the biggest threat to the world if they become powerful, though they are weak at the moment, thank God.

All other sects of if Islam are generally progressive. The biggest proof is that there are Islamic countries that are democratic, or even undemocratic, that don't follow the Wahhabi Islam and pose less of a threat to the West. Muslim scientists, influential figures, Nobel Prize winners even today when people talk about Islam, they need to know what sect of Islam are they discussing.

They need to know what part of the Islamic world they are discussing, and more importantly discuss the causes of that. Yes, it is partly Islamic regressive undemocratic Wahhabi and their ideology, and Muslims absolutely. Nonetheless, the West has played a part in making Islam regressive. Our biggest and number one ally is Saudi Arabia since 1930s and the support for Arab dictators.

The Wahhabi ideology has also made it harder to win the war against Islamic radical Wahhabi terrorism, ISIS, AL- Nusra, and so on. They are all Wahhabi.

The right way to judge Islam as a faith is if it is progressive in the 21st century. We must focus on the people, not just on undemocratic countries, undemocratic Wahhabi Islamic countries, or democratic Islamic countries. Because there are certainly non-Muslim countries that are undemocratic even though they pose a less threat then Wahhabi Islam, that does not mean this will explain to us whether Christianity or any other religion is progressive in the 21st century.

Tunisia is a perfect example of that—it was undemocratic Islamic country, but the people changed this and today Tunisia is a democratic Islamic country. In my view, this a comprehensive discussion about progressive or regressive Islam in the 21st century.

All the world must also unite, not blame all sects of Islam, and unite with all other Muslims who follow different sects of Islam in order to defeat this regressive Wahhabi Islam ideology. Otherwise, Islam will not remain progressive in the 21st century, even in Europe or the whole world, if Wahhabi Islam becomes powerful. Wahhabi Islam is regressive in the 21st century, while Islam as a religion and other sects of Islam are progressive in the 21st century.

Printed in Great Britain
by Amazon